FROM ROCK
To Fireworks

A Photo Essay
by Gary W. Davis

Children's Press

A Division of Grolier Publishing
New York London Hong Kong Sydney
Danbury, Connecticut

Created and Developed by The Learning Source

Designed by Josh Simons

Acknowledgments: We would like to thank Donna Grucci Butler and the Fireworks by Grucci staff for their technical assistance and hospitality. Their help is greatly appreciated.

Photo Credits: Bob Egan/The Learning Source: cover (background), 9 (left), 10-19, 21-26, 28 (inset), back cover; Brick Institute of America: 8, 9 (inset); Ed Harp/Unicorn Stock Photos: 4; Keith Manis/Manis Photography: cover (inset), 1, 3, 5, 6, 7, 20, 25, 27, 28, 29, 30-31, 32; Keith Manis/Manis Photography/Carl Santoro Fireworks by Grucci: 32 (middle left).

Note: The actual making of fireworks varies from manufacturer to manufacturer. The process described in this book is representative of one way of making fireworks today.

Library of Congress Cataloging-in-Publication Data
Davis, Gary W. (Gary William), 1946-
          From rock to fireworks : a photo essay / by Gary W. Davis.
          p. cm. — (Changes)
          Summary: Traces the process of making fireworks, from mining the minerals to manufacturing the shells.
          ISBN 0-516-20739-3 (lib. bdg.)   0-516-20364-9 (pbk.)
          1. Fireworks—Juvenile literature. [1. Fireworks.]
I. Title. II. Series: Changes (New York, N.Y.)
P300.D38   1997
662'.1—dc21   97-25657 CIP
                                     AC

Bursts of color streaming and sparkling . . .

. . . booms and bangs thundering through the sky . . .

. . . help us celebrate in a really BIG way.

Of course they do—they're fireworks!

But where do fireworks come from?

Fireworks start as rocks in limestone caves.
Miners dig out the rocks and send them off
to a gunpowder factory.

There, a few other ingredients are added. Machines grind and mix everything into gunpowder, which is then taken to the fireworks plant.

Fireworks are dangerous, so the plant is far away from people's homes. Workers cannot smoke, wear metal jewelry, or do anything else that might make a spark.

Anyone entering the plant must touch this copper plate. Copper removes static electricity from a person's body.

TOUCH!
STATIC DISSIPATING
PAD BEFORE ENTERING
BUILDING

Inside, the gunpowder is sifted to get rid of lumps. So are other powders. Some will give the fireworks color. Others will help them explode.

A worker mixes the
smooth powders with
water and pours
everything . . .

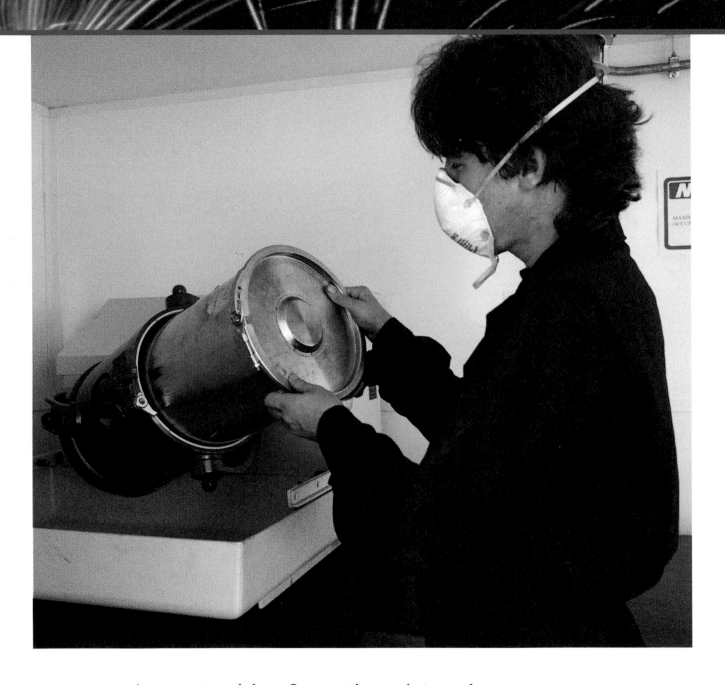

. . . into a tumbler. Soon the mixture becomes
soft dough.

The dough is cut into different shapes. These little round ones will explode into huge, colorful flowers.

Other dough shapes may become comets or shooting stars.
Some will even burst into more than one shape and color.

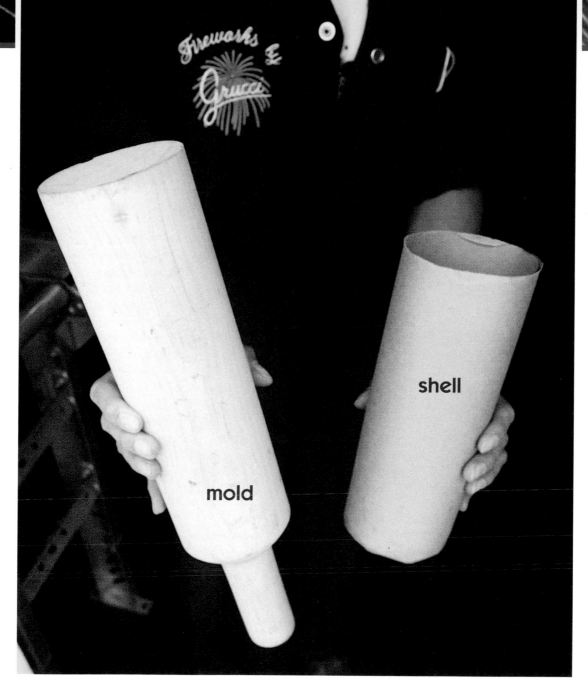

mold

shell

Cardboard is wrapped around wooden molds
to make shells. Shells are the special tubes
that help carry the fireworks into the sky.

Now, special noisemakers that add all the booms and bangs get packed into the shells.

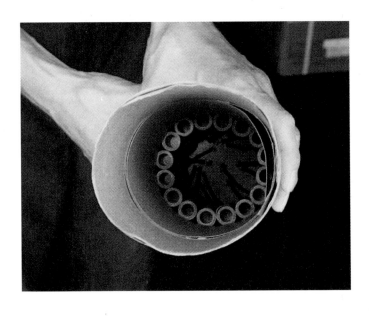

So do the pieces of dough. What goes in and how the pieces are placed will give each firework its shape, color, and sound.

A worker puts more gunpowder in the bottom of the shell to give it lift. Then on go two fuses and a layer of brown wrapping paper.

Next comes one more fuse that will light
the gunpowder, and finally . . .

. . . the finished shells go onto racks to dry.

For safety, the shells are stored in trailers that are surrounded by mounds of sand. If an accident sets off the shells, the sand will keep the explosion from spreading.

Sometimes a fireworks show needs special effects. This one is called a set piece. When lit, the name **PETER** will glow with burning tubes of color.

Set pieces are created for many kinds of events.
What holiday do you think this one is for?

Before a show, workers move the fireworks to a set-up area. One by one, the fireworks are loaded into special metal launchers.

It takes many hours to prepare for a show. Each firework must go off at a certain time and in exactly the right order.

Finally, wires are run to connect all the different launchers to a control panel.

The panel will send the electrical signals
that light the fuses to launch the fireworks.

At last . . .

FLASH!

BANG!

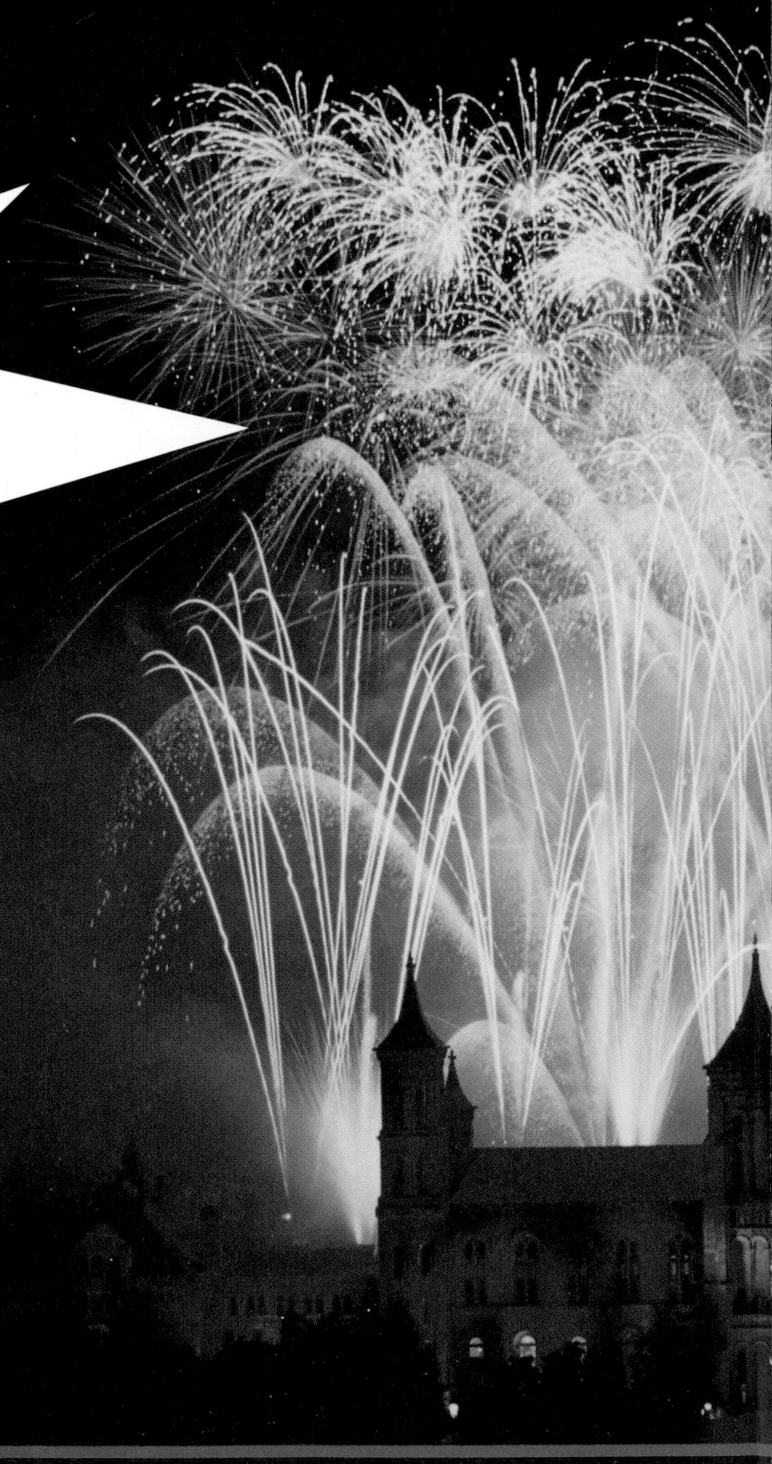

KABOOM!

It's Show Time!

31

There are many different types of fireworks.
Each has its own special shape and color.
Here are a few examples.

 CHRYSANTHEMUM

 WEEPING WILLOW

 PEONY

 TITANIUM SALUTES

 PALM TREE

 BLUE CHRYSANTHEMUM WITH PALM TREE